For Daughters Who Walk Out Like Sons

# For Daughters Who Walk Out Like Sons

## Komal Mathew

## ZONE 3 PRESS

Zone 3 Press
Austin Peay State University
Box 4565 Clarksville, TN. 37044
www.zone3press.com

Book design by Patrick Gosnell
Cover Illustration © Upasana Agarwal

Printed in the United States of America

Library of Congress Cataloging-in-Publication Data
Names: Mathew, Komal, 1982- author.
Title: For daughters who walk out like sons / Komal Mathew.
Description: Clarksville, TN : Zone 3 Press, [2021]
Identifiers: LCCN 2021027201 (print) | LCCN 2021027202 (ebook) | ISBN
9781733150552 (paperback) | ISBN 9781733150569 (ebook)
Subjects: LCGFT: Poetry.
Classification: LCC PS3613.A82628 F67 2021  (print) | LCC PS3613.A82628
(ebook) | DDC 811/.6--dc23
LC record available at https://lccn.loc.gov/2021027201
LC ebook record available at https://lccn.loc.gov/2021027202

# CONTENTS

*Do not be afraid, for I am with you;*
*I will bring your children from*
        *the east*
*and gather you from the west.*
*I will say to the north, "Give them up!"*
*And to the south, "Do not hold*
        *them back."*
*Bring my sons from afar*
*and my daughters from the ends*
*of the earth—*

-Isaiah 43:4-6

# I.

# FOR THE SHEPHERD WHO IS ALSO THE PATH THE SUN MAKES IN DAYTIME

A good shepherd is a wonder in contrapposto, an artist
mapping the Serengeti with kingdom lines.

A good shepherd angles a lion's eye, traps gazelles
in dry fields, copies a cheetah's spots one leg at a time.

A good shepherd does not give you stones
when you ask for toast, does not ask you to work

without a burning bush—but owns a gate, uses a gate, pulls
the weeds and leaves the wheat on an altar of choices.

A good shepherd is a prince of peace when terror finds its full echo,
a creator in the wild where a predator, providentially, becomes prey.

## BIRTHDAY GAMES

Before the sun hits, there is a piñata, the sprinkling
and gushing of gifts, musical chairs, round and round
as voices mouth a melody for cake. There is a donkey
kid who breathes in the icing and licks the bottom
of the candles before asking. There is also the donkey
and its tail, red eyes marking his own surprise
for missing parts, this distinct part of him that left
and never returned. Still, each kid walks up proud,
dons on the blindfold, and becomes an instant
cheat. Can we fix what we can't see? The sliver of light
tempts. *You can't peek,* someone big says. *Make sure
you close your eyes.* A small scrunched face, growls: *Why
can't I do what I want to do!* And we all become beasts.

# AN AMERICAN

Every Diwali, I explain
to my friends at school
why I am so tired—*garba*
*it's like dancing—pujas? I guess*
*like praying—*

I explain in fragments
because even we don't know
why we wash statues with milk,
why worshipping God takes
so many coats. I don't ask,

just sit beside my mother
when she sings. My sister and I
watch our father struggle
to cross his legs; his laughter
resting on his lifted knees.

He closes his eyes, pretending
to pray. We believe my mother
made this temple herself,
found pictures and tiny murtis, gold
coins with Shiva, rice and turmeric

stored in tiny steel jars. Only she knows
where everything goes and how to use it.
I have sat at that temple many times,
looking at Krishna's blue face
and pleasing smile framed inside

where life is easy—
My mother tells me he is blue
because he is so dark; *we would not be*
*able to see his face otherwise,* she says.
Every time I close my eyes to pray,

I see Jesus on that cross and taste
pennies. His blond face like the girl
in music class who told me not to
take the Lord's name *in vain.*
I feel guilty wanting to

have stew and tuna sandwiches
instead of khichri. So when my Ba
showed up at school this afternoon
in her maroon and gold sari, and called
my name, I didn't answer.

I walked past her to the car, slid
between my sister and her white friend.
I wanted to believe that I was still
American, hiding in the backseat
like a crumpled sari.

# DRESSING FOR DIWALI

In the beginning, you gave me this skin.
This brown speckled hyper—
       that's what they say—pigmentation.
This dry sand, flour-dusted calves
from sitting Indian style, a familiar place
behind my knees: a black fan of skin.

This is what you gave me
after the garden full of sun:
       a paisley pattern
(A glory to God? For these dappled things?)
       this cross-stitch in goldless seams.

◆

My first confession:

hands piled on my calf

birthmark

barely covered.

I tried to tell you

before you noticed.

I tried to tell you

my mother believes

it was the radish

sandwiches she ate.

She says they stain

so easily.

◆

Here are the tears of things:

On Diwali, my mother hems the frayed edges
of her old cotton sari for me—
timidly tucking in the excess to form a clean,
deep-seated seam, trying to make it all look
right. Across the room, I shout
       *stop*
*don't—*
                 I want to wear
*the new one!*

&#9670;

She tells us stories of a god
at the beginning, making our skin
like dosas and sambar,
ready hands on a hot stove.

This god toasts sesame seeds
in a metal pot. When they burn,
as they often do, he tosses them
*to the south*, she says—their graves made
before they were born. When he tries again,
our persistent maker of coconut chutneys turns
the heat off too soon and we are left
with everything as it was created—raw and white.

Here, in this story, we are supposed to believe that
we were made well: a perfect skin (can *we* say that?)
after continents left to god's sowing and throwing. Tale
stories, a village of histories, a long oral tradition of one
epic after another, a story hoping to feel like the middle
of my parents' bed, the smell of cardamom in the kitchen
during afternoon chai breaks, summers at the shaded pool

where all I can remember is one thing: changing
into my black bathing suit and trying to *cover, cover,*
*cover*—let's not make this into a skin story, too—
But what about my legs? Compliments on being fair
and lovely? What about North *and* South India?
And here? What about the celebration of places
that taste like yogurt but smell like curry?

◆

On Diwali, my mother folds her face, fixes what I want.
My lips are too dark—blush on me, and I remember
this is the garden:               a garment of choice

when you have eighteen shades of shadow. I wanted You
to dress me—even if everything around me is white
lights—to spread all Your colors on my face,
smear my lips and darken my eyes.

# THE FIRST TIME

The first time I heard
the story of the prodigal son,
I was in college and always jealous,

imagining him in his father's robe
and ring, eating all that calf.
*Dishonor is worse than death.*

I believe it because I'm Indian
and hear so many stories about
unkept marriages and children

who leave their parents in homes
where they don't serve Gujarati
meals. My father still makes me

promise to take care of him,
even if I have a better choice,
even if the food is not that bad.

This time I hear the parable
in my friend's living room,
sitting on a couch cornered

by her piano and fireplace.
Her father is describing love
as if it were always good.

[romantic theme increases in volume and dynamics]

The scene is simple. Two horses fall in love over apples—
When I say I want to be consumed, I remember that women die
by fire, our women, at higher rates than men. Standing next to
a stove, throwing a thousand mustard seeds. I think you know
I mean hurry and halt. Take a penny and please leave
a penny: charity of mind starts with the benefit of action.
See what I did there? I'm still at the beginning of this romance.
Tell me that's the way it works before I go and you go
with me, ambitious, to the beginning of many deaths. Who could
trust the future with a past like that? Who could see love
as anything else than an all-consuming fire?

# EVERYTHING I'VE HEARD FROM THE GOD OF NATIONS

You didn't say love
the way I made it:
a near, new thing.
You said abide
like long stanzas
like a memory
with many owners.

You didn't say love
when I put on armor,
reminding myself of soft
pashminas, counterfeits
with ends. You said abide,
so how important is it
to protect my head?

You didn't say love
like I've heard it
out of a lover's mouth,
a blood orange love.
How could you
say it another way?

You said abide,
so what can I say back?
*Of course, yes, always—*
like a tradition
like an Eastern thing.

# SATYAGRAHA FOR THIN FEET

Like the army you were converting—
you took my people and their thin feet
and led them to a salty sea.

To give them truth, you dressed holiness
as a 240-mile braid towards a sorted beach,
lifted them like long grain rice, shaky

before an anointing. How was I to know
that this was a miracle? Thousands walking
from one sacrificial place to another.

When it passed down to me, I did not inherit
the holiness of shifting from sea to salt, child to priest.
I became heir to my mother and her garnet ring.

Thinking I owned her, I pulled her fingers back,
pushed into her ring. I found a place for me
to put my cheek: a *colonization* of skin and blood.

Then later, my mother held my hand, unpacked
our lunch at Lavender Pond. She let go
because I let go: a *symbiosis* of skin and blood.

And suddenly I owned my body and didn't have to
look back. What was I doing but starting my own march
into a place of peace and rest, moving toward sacrifice?

What was I doing but converting my own body, changing
because I was free from the glory of one hand? *Satyagraha*
when I leave good places with thin feet, walking

into found places. *Satyagraha* when I no longer belong
to the mutable sea. *Satyagraha* now that I am Yours,
and You are mine. Your glorious, holy body of boats.

# II.

# THE RETURN

*The finding has the losing in the background, the returning has the leaving under its cloak.*
*–Henri J.M. Nouwen, The Return of the Prodigal Son*

When you come out of exile, do they celebrate you—
Do they thicken milk with sugar and add crushed cashews?

Do they lay it out with ghee and gold vark like a thin carpet
welcoming a king god? Do they feed you with rows of candles,

a praise of small lights? Do they celebrate that evil failed
and goodness won, that you changed after leaving

after covering a wound, after coming home
to wear what your father wanted you to wear?

◆

In the beginning, the [home] already existed.
The [home] was with God.
The [home] was God.

Then God said, "Let the [homes] beneath the sky flow together in one place, so dry ground may appear." And that is what happened. God called the dry ground ["freedom"] and the [homes "community"].

◆

The surprise isn't that the son would leave, desiring land
in a new community. The surprise isn't that he would win
after losing, that he would return ashamed of dark corners.
The surprise isn't that the good father would give the son
a party that takes more of his wealth. It isn't the older, bitter
gate that opened wide, the brother who protested
this grace upon grace upon grace.

The surprise is that the prodigal son accepts all of it—
the long safe road home, the hug, the meat off the bone.

◆

How does anyone come back without going?
Go without being sent? Send without hearing first?
How does anyone hear without being told and told and told?

How does anyone tell without first believing?
(Am I who my father says I am?) How does anyone believe
without being called?

> We are down the road, past the main road, over
> the far border—living in a wilderness but marching
> towards a new land. How can a father call his son

when the son is freely living on dry ground, pacing across
every red road as if the seas were eternally parted?

◆

There are questions that take sharp
rights, questions that have limits,
questions that curve slowly, ringing
into ripples. There are questions that go
nowhere, turn around and ask *Where was I*
*going in the first place? Who was I*
*trying to see?*

◆

In the beginning, the [inheritance] already existed.

The [inheritance] was with God.

The [inheritance] was God.

Then God said, "Let there be a space between the [homes], to separate the [homes] of the heavens from the [homes] of the earth." And that is what happened. God made this space to separate the [homes] of the earth from the [homes] of the heavens. God called the space ["poverty"].

◆

*Beta*, did you know
that you have a home?
You stayed. You obeyed.
Did you know that this home
is where you want to be?
Did you know that I also left
a field for you—

◆

You've been carrying the box for so long
you think it's a good idea to stop
and place it on someone else's doorstep.
When your neighbor realizes it's not
the ripe oranges she ordered, she will
pick it up and hold it close to her
chest, for you. Its weight won't crush her.
Though it will require a pull from her
wrist and a shoulder stretch, a squeeze
from her heart—through the door until,
days later, maybe years, she will pass it back
like new: a package waiting to be carried,
the brown flap of the box folded to make
a smile, for a friend, so sweet and so kind.

◆

My grandmother's skin is a moving river, rippling
from her thumb to wrist to her elbows, falling
toward her wedding ring and gold bracelets. Short clings
announce her knees' desire for hands. What I love most
is the stories she tells when she makes dhokla. She stirs
without the pinky or the thumb, a three-finger salute
to chickpea flour and Eno, repeating lines of a young bride
to taste and see if it is the same as last week's. She beats
the batter before it rises, making sure it knows nothing
lasts forever. Her tired hands stir and pour and heap
until we are full and ready to return home.

◆

If I am the clay
and you are the one
that gives gold
on gold on gold
(somebody has to)
If I make myself
into a deep dish,
ready for the pour
If I ask you
to take care of me—
in bigger houses
and faster cars, in and out
of tunnels, would you
make me into something
little, what you could hold
in both of your hands?

◆

Now, I see—

the hands may be yours,

but the feet are mine.

You are reading

the way fathers run

toward a daughter's palm,

how daughters walk out

like sons

and return,

their feet, a beauty

before mountains.

# III.

# HOME, AFTER HOMES

1.

A bronze cross from your father's coffin hovers
over our headboard. *Don't start with the dead first,*
your father told you, so we start small and alive
like we were just planted into the earth.

2.

You don't want a house with a yard
because weekends aren't meant for work,
so we grow gray plants in a city condo.
You get up early—like your father did—
to make me egg sandwiches. You measure ice,
slice bananas and persimmons into a blender,
into shapes—diamonds, toy blocks, caution cones.

3.

I learn how to call you every day, to ask what we're planting
and why and when and for how long. In my old home,
a black statue of Ganesh sits with crossed legs in the foyer.
Some Americans keep idols in their pockets, my father tells me.
Even the president, *for luck.* Pruning seems like the right thing,
so I look for someplace to put a different clue to all who enter.

4.

This Is An Indian Home—but all I want is our wedding picture
and my grandmother's small bowl of salt. Each night, I close
one eye at a time, trying to see who we really are—
the left, the right, left, right—eyes trapping gusts of wind,
until I see you, my love, with three children, until I see you
in a clean home with no yard.

# AFTER THE HONEYMOON, HOME

1.
I've been cleaning all day, wiping
countertops, sills, and tops of TVs.

Sperm can live in you for three days,
you remind me. *I know,* like dust
collecting on your favorite book, I tell you.

2.
We've been killing
my mother's mint plant
for weeks, taking turns
being parents:
water, my milk
a small ledge, a crib—
an offer of all our pleasant places.
Now, it's another Tuesday
and we have made a dry
Medusa mess. I shower,
think about adoption,
take a three-mile walk
before noticing two dogs
shepherding one hundred
goats in the park—chosen, elected
to eat invasive kudzu, where
a mint plant grows wildly
without us.

3.
Before you were born,
I saw both of you
as toddlers
kneeling

under a window
of reds and yellows
of Jesus the Shepherd.
I think you will love

lambs like he did—
in foreign places
in stained-glass windows
those almost shattered pieces.

4.
The world gets smaller
when you're in the city.
The city gets smaller
when you're planting
tulips in your backyard—

imagining yourself a sower,
a gardener of two little figures
of speech, formed in a small
frame of dust—
          *(oh, unimaginable God!)*
you both came and stayed
for more than one night.

# HOME, AFTER BABIES

In the park today, a couple tied a rope
between two stubborn trees. They wound
the thread, making it stronger with each full
twist. When she stepped out, her foot shook
down that thin string aisle. Then, in one hop,
before she reached the end, his foot was flat
against the back of the red-striped cable.
His other foot did dynamic stretches—
a pointed toe, a forward lunge, a thriving
tango—as if he still were leading
a company of admirers.

# TAKING OUT THE TRASH IN CALCUTTA

Anyplace is better
than outside of a hospital.

Bags of needles,
blunt by skin and vein,
buckets of lungs, hung heavy
on the hands of a white missionary, crying:
> *Life from heaven, let the children be asleep.*
> *Let their thunder be feet away.*
But they do not listen, do not hear.

He holds the bag higher, hitting small hands
that scratch down his shirt, *not the bag,*
*not the bag,* his head to the sky, collapsing
at the look of teething children—running,
smiling, bits of flesh on their chins.

◆

While you were growing in me, you were a balloon
with good helium, stretching the corners of this small
earth, creating space out of a dark nothing
the way the universe does, making known
what's invisible, what's grand. *It's not fair*

yell my other two. I want to sit on your lap.
Want space. *Make space*
they plead. It's not fair.
*I'm big now. We're big kids now.* How strange:

some gifts grow
to be fishers and grievers

of men —*what is man, what is man*—
to grow half-full and half-empty
wanting to be made and kept
like a jar of saffron
that bleeds deep and wide
that finds something sweet
in someone's warm milk.

◆

In someone's warm milk forms
a belly, a kidney, a wide lap inside and out
of another woman—perhaps from Calcutta—
feeling known around masses, realizing wherever
she goes, a child goes with her.

Here, there is a purple lavender bush and a wasp
that won't let go outside our front door.

My children are on the floor
cheeks hugging one another, screaming
at the sound of the alarm ringing. I left
and returned quickly to a flood
of sound, a felt massacre of fear
in my children's hands.

Forget kite flying with friends earlier that day,
hide and seek, pizza they folded, chocolate
syrup left on the plastic tablecloths, milk and carrot
birthday cake: all the remains of the living—
forget it all—there is a dying inside
everywhere.

# FLIGHT

Though my love for you didn't end
because the singing ended, the lullaby
moved to a wind that promised a nest
for a grounded mama bird. For one day,

her hard-earthed belly did not fly. One day
of low hops and wobbles. I need you to see
to hear this bird's morning song, ceaseless
in the count. *Do you see?* This bird did not carry

a wedding band's grief, sweet swollen
sugar blood, heartbeats that grow louder
and fall longer. A body in detour.
My love, the blues is a lullaby—

*please stay with me—*
when there is one egg to care for,
one egg outside of the body,
breathing and becoming whole.

# SWIM LESSONS

The God who is there
took and divided your breath,
which you held

small gifts
like a creation story.

The God who is there
gave you a clean push of space
which you sifted

under growing waters
like you were dividing the Nile.

*Child!*
what have you left behind—
a stretched summer day?

a tiptoe on warm pavement?
a clear view of the sun?

What won't you do
to prove
than still water

you want more
more than soft steps?

# GIFTS FOR A BEAUTIFUL BODY

*-after Ta-Nehisi Coates and to my son*

Who am I to tell you now
what was given to me

(by my mother
and my mother's mother)?

A gold bracelet, engraved
with my name, announcing

God's ornament, a visible body
covered in star-studded cotton.

I wanted to give you gold, myrrh,
and frankincense, but your cry

kept circling the dim room, hungry
and fragrant. I needed your faithfulness

of breath. Your skipping and pedaling
feet, your feet *(Oh Mary!)* of ages.

I would have to lie to tell you
that death always comes

like precious stones. Some are slashed,
some buried, so many given invisibility

like a gift—perhaps the only way to see
a body is with your own eyes.

Perhaps the only way to see a whole body
is to see one coming out of you.

You survived before you lived,
but I still listen for heartbeats

in arched places, anxious when people
walk around you like broken branches.

Blessed be the one who hears you cry out
like a million pressed stones —

jasper, turquoise, emerald with gold —
and uncovers your breath of bees.

Blessed be the one who sees you on the sidewalk,
migrating, and declares you good.

# GRAVE CLOTHES

First a fragrance
filled our house:
honeysuckle sweat
soaked in the doors
you touched, the nail
in the tulip garden
where you noticed
the dropping moon
and longed to see it
(once and for all)
I will put on your dark
grave clothes
and wonder why
I feel bound to your body
the gray-dry skin of you
the barrenness of feet
that now looks odd
in daylight, odd
to anyone alive.

# AFTER A LONG WALK, MY DAUGHTER ASKS
# WHY WE CAN'T JUST DIE TOGETHER

1.
We have looked at pool covers and rusty drains.
We have searched red bushes for thorns, scraped
an elbow on a brick step.

We have announced *no doggie, no doggie, not over here.*
Then ran with heads turned back, our long thick
Indian hair blocking our view.

We have witnessed iridescent bubbles lit in the soapy sun, waiting:
*Right left right left* stop. Then danced on the yellow rippled ramps
leading us to new tar roads.

My smallest known tour guide, you are not tired.
You are never tired—
my soreless child, my fossil
finder—my bones
splintering each year you grow
stronger and faster.

2.
We are on the corner going somewhere set in stone,
and you lunge towards Spring Street, your small arm
pulling towards the curved walkway, your neck beaked
like a soldier pulling a flag to the ground—*this is the way.*
I pull and lunge towards Church, lining up one foot
in front of the other while you keep turning,
loving nothing carved from this world.

3.
This is important: the tradition of never finishing
the ritual—a bedtime routine, a coffee pot
on the hot plate again and again, the thin glass
that always breaks, but if you do it on purpose,

41

(say for a wedding), it will mean something.
It will mean something if it never ends

like all the blue fireworks we watch to lighten your face
and darken my shoulder. A memory buried so deep
in the room of our living, that later you will believe
there are brighter places that feel like our home.

4.
To go separately means that either I walk behind
or you—like a man rushing through morning
pedestrians goes into a building, up the stairs,
to an office that's really a room made of boxes
and tape. It means like a man, you will go first
and then we can just forget about our walk,
Argentina in the summer, the Micah clock. The stories
will stay on the shelf. To go separately means one of us
will die breathing in. It means one of us will walk
on cracks hoping for a heart swallow. It means the back
of your earring will still be lost and forget about six
or seven or eight. It will mean one day folding into fifty years—
*So why can't we go together?* The reasons are wide and deep and high,
but we will go separately while one of us waits
at the bus stop—*Will it be you?*—
one of us will start drinking
coffee to remember that plan we had
on the calendar, to go for a walk that leads us
to a coffee shop where I could tell you:

I don't love you like the small things
you carry in your pocket.
I don't love you like the things
you carry on your back.
I love you like you could live forever.

# IV.

# IN THE GARDEN: A TOMB

*When the soldiers crucified Jesus, they took his clothes, dividing them into four shares, one for each of them, with the undergarment remaining. This garment was seamless, woven in one piece from top to bottom.*

-John 19:23

### 1.

It hasn't happened to me personally, but I've heard,
I've read about the ripping of shirts and shorts,
the narrow alley at the mall, the dark rooms in every house-

boat, city condo, white house. I don't know personally,
but it seems like there is no soul in the well anymore,
no little girl that can play alone on a private street.

Though I don't know that room personally, I am careful
opening the front door at noon when my kids are home—
whatever you are selling, others are trying too—

(Did you know that—to sell girls like her?) I don't know
personally, but I know it's not wise to go to the park alone
with my three young kids; there are not enough hands

to keep them all safe or the others that swing in low secret
waves, squinting up to the sun. I don't personally know anyone
who doesn't think about the ripping and the dark room. *If you don't*

*see me,* if you get lost, remember to press the button with the star,
find a crowd. Look first for a momma, then a *masi,* a papa,
but never just a man alone. I tell them, knowing this is personal,

knowing that God will at last remain silent for any man
who's decided to do publicly what he has been thinking privately.
I don't want you to be in that dark bruised-purple room.

2.

Your first words
are leaf pirouettes, a ring
on a glass counter, my best
and worst—an echo of my ways—

Your words are a silent lonely work, Isaac
down the road, pulled faster than he can walk.
And you sway, singing *no, no, no.*

3.

He is your only Son. She is my only daughter.

Am I to believe that this is the trouble
you meant—this disrobing, stripping
of before and after? That you would
be the Father of this kind of pruning
where there is a field of stones
to aim for every part of you?
That you would open and lay bare
your knees and shoulders and high thigh,
that you would be willing to allow dirtier nails
to dig up this earth that you created, this earth
you created by tearing a hole and speaking into it?

        4. Eve to her son:
I am not worried about my sin
but yours, your sin that sleeps
for three years after a faithful
fifteen—the full snail of you
that no one knows. Do you know
what I was doing fifteen years ago?
I was cradling a city as if it had tiny
fingers and toes. I was in love
with the work of my brown hands.
I loved the law and not the person
it was supposed to love. Now, you
without memory of being born, see
only the full, fruit trees. Open your eyes,
son: the apple is ripe and ready
for the shaken eye. You have a memory now,
so I pray you will see: everything isn't ours
to have, to hold, and pursue.

5. Cain to Abel:

I know I was young, but I was with God walking, talking with him
in the cool of the day, watching him draw an august gesture, in damp sand—
a design for tic-tac-toe or perhaps hangman?—I didn't know

how to play then, with words, with a winner and a loser, with the knowledge
of good and evil, but I saw a line drawn just for me, pointing me
to a choice, not my flavor of speech, protesting what she took from the garden
and what I could take from your grave.

6.

When they come, they take the front door first,
then your whole home—the broken chairs, the wide
table, your linens. They take the firewood,
the wedding jewelry, your hand lotion
and water glasses. But your clothes.
Your clothes are the last things they take;
your clothes are your last earthly possession.

7.

Rebekah: *Why is this happening to me?*

Moses: *Why, Lord, why have you brought trouble on this people?*
     *Is this why you sent me?*

Naomi: *Why call me Naomi? The LORD has afflicted me;*
     *the Almighty has brought misfortune upon me.*

Saul: *Why have you not answered your servant today?*

Job: *Why have you made me your target?*

Habakkuk: *Why are you silent while the wicked swallow up*
     *those more righteous than themselves?*

Jeremiah: *Why did I ever come out of the womb*
     *to see trouble and sorrow and to end my days in shame?*

Jesus: *My God, my God, why have you forsaken me?*

8.

The Living Water is thirsty? After all the sin, He was thirsty?

9.

Let me be clear: He was naked
before He died. All but one man
left, but the women—four of them—
stayed at the cross, hoping to cover Him
in burial clothes. Did you honor them
as they honored you? Let me

be clear: you were naked but not alone—
the women, did they know

that they would die too? Should I trust
the linen you have made
for me to wear?

10.

Someone somewhere is teaching me
how to be vulnerable, to be a julienned
carrot turned stew, a meatloaf kneaded
in a blue kitchen. There are buffets, you know,
where you can find everything on display.
You can find pineapple and Italian dressing and everyone
loves it because everything is available in every aisle—
please say something. Are you hungry? Are you thirsty?
Say something about my furrowed brow, about my turning
to the side to sleep now, not on my stomach, not again. The stomach,
the curl, the turning inside, the disappearing belly, the turning into
pride the way a man says *I'm tired* or *That's right.*

11.

All day, she has been wailing over what's gone—a ball, a broccoli floret,

her yellow duck lost on a sidewalk. She's been drinking new cups of trembling.

Somehow we are getting up and walking and finding new clothes—

like He did—to wear. Sweet girl, *celebrate:* the old garment is gone,

but the tomb is empty. *Celebrate.* The linen is on the floor.

*Celebrate.* The curtain is torn. *Celebrate.* Somewhere

He went and found new clothes, new clothes

to show us that He is alive, to show how His faithfulness looks

like summer in Finland

where darkness doesn't know how long to stay—

12.

Should I trust this linen,
this new veil—

There is no other covering,
you say—Father, *forgive me*
for the places
I have sat and known:
there is no place for you
to lay your head.
Father, forgive me

I didn't notice
the splendid place
the shelter under
your straw hat.

# NOTES

"For the Shepherd Who Is Also the Path the Sun Makes in Daytime," based on Psalm 23, is for Ayan.

◆

In "Dressing for Diwali," the parenthetical questions refer to the line "Glory be to God for dappled things" from "Pied Beauty" by Gerard Manley Hopkins. "Here are the tears of things" is taken from Plate 27 of George Rouault's *Misere Et Guerre* collection, a series of paintings published by the Museum of Biblical Art.

◆

For some, the origin of *Diwali* ("Festival of Lights") is linked to the Sanskrit epic *Ramayana,* where King Rama returns to the city of Ayodhya after a fourteen-year exile. The people of Ayodhya lined the path with rows of lamps to welcome him home.

◆

In "The First Time," "Dishonor is worse than death" is a quote from Chapter II: 34–36 in the *Bhagavad Gita.*

◆

"[romantic theme increases in volume and dynamics]" borrows its title from a closed caption line in *Spirit: Stallion of the Cimarron* (2002).

◆

"Satyagraha for Thin Feet" was inspired by the 1930 Salt Satyagraha led by Mahatma Gandhi. The march lasted 24 days (about 240 miles) from Ahmedabad to Dandi Beach, where thousands harvested salt to protest Britain's salt tax. Prior to the march, in a letter to the British Viceroy Lord Irwin, Gandhi clearly stated his ambition: "to convert the British people through nonviolence and thus make them see the wrong they have done to India."

♦

"Gifts for a Beautiful Body" was inspired by Ta-Nehisi Coates' *Between the World and Me.*

♦

This book borrows language from Genesis 1:6–10, Genesis 25:22, Exodus 5:22, Ruth 1:21, 1 Samuel 14:41, Job 7:20, Habakkuk 1:13, Jeremiah 20:18, John 1:1, Matthew 27:46, and Romans 10:14–15.

# ACKNOWLEDGMENTS

When it takes over a decade to write a book, any gesture of thanks feels inadequate. Still, I would like to thank my friends, family, colleagues, classmates, and teachers who by name outnumber the words in this book. I'm deeply grateful to all of you for helping shape this writing life and the long pursuit of it, for your heartfelt encouragement and support.

To Aubrey Collins, Stephanie Dugger, Patrick Gosnell, and the Zone 3 Press team, for patiently answering my questions and devoting your time and expertise in a particularly hard season. To Paige Lewis, for choosing this story from the shadows and giving my voice a cover. To Karen Anh-Wei Lee and Aimee Nezhukumatathil, for your generosity of words to the world and me. To Upasana Agarwal for sharing your talent and wonder with me. To the kind editors of the following publications in which these poems, sometimes in different versions, first appeared:

*Beloit Poetry Journal:* "In the Garden: A Tomb"

*Chattahoochee Review:* "Everything I've Heard from the God of Nations," "Satyagraha for Thin Feet," and "Home, After Homes"

*Coal Hill Review:* "The First Time"

*Crazyhorse:* "Birthday Games"

*Diode Poetry Journal:* "The Return"

*The Missouri Review:* "After a Long Walk, My Daughter Asks Why We Can't Just Die Together"

*Narrative:* "[romantic theme increases in volume and dynamics]," "Gifts for a Beautiful Body," "Flight," and "Grave Clothes"

*The New Republic:* "An American"

*Poetry:* "For the Shepherd Who Is Also the Path the Sun Makes in Daytime"

*Prairie Schooner:* "Dressing for Diwali" and "After the Honeymoon, Home"

*Third Coast:* "Taking Out the Trash in Calcutta"

Special thanks to Thomas Lux for reminding me that writing poetry was both a call and a choice. To Barbara Schwartz, my perceptive friend and faithful editor, for holding this manuscript with me in all its forms and joining me in the workroom (for years!) until it was ready. To Jenny Sadre-Orafai, the best cheerleader and friend, for inspiring me to champion others when I write.

To Deanna Davis, Namratha George, Christie Holben, Nisy Narayana Jaya, Elitsa Naumova-Falade, Kristy Orisma, Lena Shah, Renuka Thorne, Sajini Varghese, Amanda Wallace, Yashira Willis, and many other sister friends. Thank you for caring about my flourishing in every season.

To my parents, who raised me to know that daughters are a blessing and still find ways to protect and celebrate us. To my sister, who knows what it means to joyfully sing a country duet in parts with your most loyal friend. Thank you for all the undeserved hype.

To my husband Lance, for steering me toward gratitude in all things, for listening to my insecurities and walking me out from under them. Every day, there is more to love about you. This is for our children and our children's children—and for His glory that could never be described in my small story or theirs—

—and yet, dear reader, He knows you, sees you, and cares.